SCIENCE PROJECTS

THE ENVIRONMENT

Robert Snedden

Photography by
Chris Fairclough

RSVP
RAINTREE
STECK-VAUGHN
PUBLISHERS
A Steck-Vaughn Company

Austin, Texas

Library of Congress Cataloging-in-Publication Data
Snedden, Robert.
The environment / Robert Snedden.
     p.   cm.—(Science Projects)
     Includes bibliographical references and index.
     Summary: Describes various elements that make up an environment, including the carbon cycle, the water cycle, and food chains.
     ISBN 0-8172-4964-8
     1. Environmental sciences—Juvenile literature.
     [1. Environmental sciences. 2. Ecology.]
     I. Fairclough, Chris, ill. II. Title.
     III. Series.
     GE115.S64   1998
     577—dc21   97-46789

Printed in Italy. Bound in the United States.
1 2 3 4 5 6 7 8 9 0 02 01 00 99 98

Picture acknowledgments:
The publishers would like to thank the following for permission to reproduce their pictures:
Bruce Coleman: pages 15, 26 (both), 33, 36; **Ecoscene:** page 9; **Getty Images:** front cover, pages 6, 12, 18, 23, 24, 28, 30, 40; **NHPA:** page 39; **Science Photo Library:** page 4.
Illustrations: Julian Baker: front cover; Stefan Chabluk: pages 5, 10, 16, 18, 20, 39.

CONTENTS

THE ENVIRONMENT

You may often have heard people saying, "We must protect the environment." What do they mean? They probably mean the countryside or the rain forests or the oceans. These are parts of the environment, but the environment is much more. Your environment is all the living and nonliving things that you come into contact with. The cars pumping out exhaust gases in your street are as much a part of your environment as are the trees in your yard.

The global environment is even larger still. It includes all the complicated relationships between living things and the nonliving world. The global environment can be divided into two parts: the physical environment, which includes all the nonliving components, such as light, water, and temperature; and the biotic, or biological environment, which includes all the living things in the environment.

The study of the relationships among living things and their environments is called ecology. Each living thing—including you—has a range of environmental conditions that suit it best. In this book we will investigate the relationships between living things and their environments. We will look at how changing their environmental conditions can affect plants and animals.

Cities are as much a part of the global environment as are tropical rain forests and grasslands.

LOOKING AT YOUR ENVIRONMENT

There are a huge number of links between you and your environment.

We share our environment with other people, such as family and friends, who can have a big influence on our behavior.

Some living things, such as the microscopic dust mite, share your environment without your even being aware of them. There may be a million of these tiny creatures living in your bed, feeding on skin flakes from your body.

The weather is a key part of our environment. It affects every aspect of our daily lives, from what we wear to what we eat and drink.

The countryside is a vital part of our environment. Farmers work the land to grow the food we need. Today, we can find foods in our supermarkets that have come from all over the world, grown in environments that may be very different from our own.

Nonliving things also play a big part in our environment. Car exhausts release huge quantities of harmful gases into the air we breathe.

ENERGY FOR LIFE

Sunlight is the ultimate source of energy for almost all living things. In one year, 10,000 times more energy reaches the earth from the sun than is used by all of the world's human population. A tiny fraction of this energy is absorbed by green plants.

Plants use the energy from the sun to power photosynthesis. Photosynthesis is the process by which green plants manufacture sugars from water and carbon dioxide. A small part of the sun's energy is stored in the sugars. Animals get their energy either by eating plants or by eating other animals that eat plants. Because green plants make food for themselves and other animals, ecologists refer to them as producers.

The energy of the sun also has other important roles to play in the environment. Without this energy it

Sunflowers are so named because they turn toward the sun. Like all green plants, they depend on sunlight to make their food.

would be too cold for life as we know it to survive. It is solar energy that powers the earth's weather systems. Solar energy heats up the atmosphere, producing currents of air, which we call winds, as warm air rises and cool air sinks. Without the sun, the wind wouldn't blow.

DID YOU KNOW?

Life can be found even at the bottom of the deepest ocean where no sunlight reaches. Bacteria survive by living around volcanic vents, on the ocean floor. They combine sulfur compounds from the vents with oxygen to release energy to make their food. The bacteria are eaten by other animals, such as 6-ft. (2-m) long tube worms, crabs, shrimp, and giant clams.

PLANTS AND LIGHT

In this experiment you can see how a plant grows to position itself to get the light it needs. It is important that you use two similar-sized plants of the same type.

1. Paint the box black, inside and out.

2. When the paint is dry, cut a large vertical opening in one side of the box.

DID YOU KNOW?

In one second the sun gives off 13 million times more energy than all the electricity used in the U.S. in a year.

3. Water both plants evenly, then put one of the plants in a well-lit spot. Turn the plant every half hour or so to make sure it gets light from all sides.

4. Cover the other plant with the box and place it so that light will shine in through the opening, perhaps on a sunny window ledge.

5. After a few hours remove the box from the plant and compare both plants. Can you see a difference? You should be able to see that the plant that was in the box has begun to point toward the light. What would happen to a plant kept in a box into which no light could enter? Block the hole and monitor the results over a month.

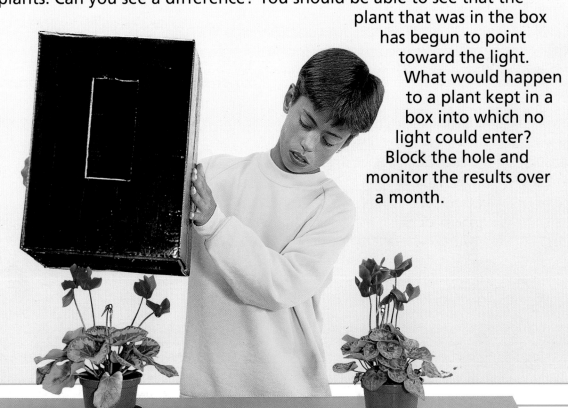

OXYGEN PRODUCERS

When life first appeared on Earth, perhaps four billion years ago, there was scarcely any oxygen in the atmosphere. Organisms evolved and were able to use photosynthesis to harness energy. Since photosynthesis produces oxygen as a by-product, the composition of the atmosphere began to change. Today, oxygen makes up about one fifth of the air we breathe. The level of oxygen in the atmosphere is maintained by plants.

When you breathe air into your lungs, oxygen enters your bloodstream and is carried to all the tissues of your body. The oxygen combines with digested food in the cells of the tissues in a process called respiration. Respiration is a little like a controlled burning of food, combining it with oxygen to release energy that can be used by your body. A by-product of respiration is a gas called carbon dioxide, which you breathe out.

COLLECTING OXYGEN

Almost all living things need oxygen to survive. In this experiment you can try to collect some of the oxygen produced by a plant.

You should be able to find the pondweed in a garden center or an aquarium supply shop. If you don't have a transparent funnel, the cut-off top of a plastic soda bottle will do instead.

MATERIALS
- 1 or 2 strands of pondweed or other green aquarium plant
- paper clips
- an aquarium
- a transparent funnel
- a test tube
- a few small pebbles
- a wooden splint
- safety matches

1. Fill the aquarium with cold water. Attach a couple of paper clips onto one end of your plant strands to weight them before placing them on the bottom of the aquarium. Make a circle of pebbles around the plant strands.

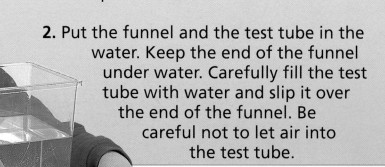

2. Put the funnel and the test tube in the water. Keep the end of the funnel under water. Carefully fill the test tube with water and slip it over the end of the funnel. Be careful not to let air into the test tube.

Oxygen is released into the air by trees, grass, and other plants. Animals, such as these cows, take in the released oxygen when they respire. The oxygen combines with food so that the animal can utilize the energy from what it eats. Animals also use oxygen, together with other chemicals, to renew their cells.

3. Place the funnel and test tube over the pondweed so that the funnel sits on the pebbles and covers the plant.

4. Leave the setup in a sunny place. It is important that the plant have access to bright light.

5. Soon you should see bubbles of gas rising from the plant into the tube. Gradually the gas will replace the water in the tube. After a few days, the tube should be nearly full of the gas.

6. Carefully remove the tube from the funnel, keeping your thumb over the end of the tube to keep the gas from escaping. Ask an adult to light the end of the splint with a match. After a moment, blow out the flame and place the glowing end of the splint in the test tube. What happens to the splint? Why do you think this happens?

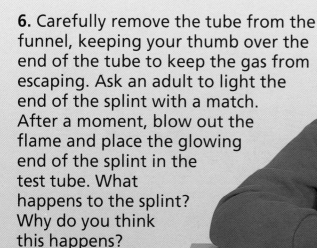

THE CARBON CYCLE

All living things use respiration to break down their food to obtain energy. Respiration normally uses oxygen and produces water and carbon dioxide. Green plants use carbon dioxide and give off oxygen during photosynthesis. Over the whole of the global environment, respiration and photosynthesis are in balance, and the amounts of carbon dioxide and oxygen in the atmosphere stay more or less constant. This natural recycling process is called the carbon cycle.

The diagram below shows how the activities of humans have upset the natural balance of the carbon cycle. Some of the heat from the sun is reflected straight back into space from the earth's surface. Carbon dioxide, and some other gases, can trap this heat in the atmosphere in a phenomenon called the greenhouse effect.

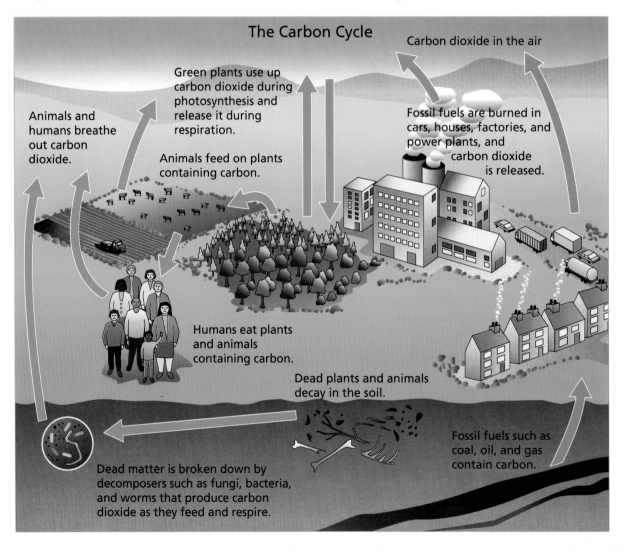

The Carbon Cycle

Carbon dioxide in the air

Green plants use up carbon dioxide during photosynthesis and release it during respiration.

Animals and humans breathe out carbon dioxide.

Fossil fuels are burned in cars, houses, factories, and power plants, and carbon dioxide is released.

Animals feed on plants containing carbon.

Humans eat plants and animals containing carbon.

Dead plants and animals decay in the soil.

Fossil fuels such as coal, oil, and gas contain carbon.

Dead matter is broken down by decomposers such as fungi, bacteria, and worms that produce carbon dioxide as they feed and respire.

The greenhouse effect keeps the earth's surface at an average temperature of about 86° F (30° C) more than it would be otherwise. The buildup of carbon dioxide in the atmosphere may be causing an increase in the greenhouse effect, which may result in an increase in the overall temperature of the earth. Environmentalists call this global warming and are afraid it will lead to unpredictable changes in the world's climates. It is by no means certain, however, that global warming is actually taking place.

A BOTTLE ENVIRONMENT

MATERIALS
- a large clear jar with a screwtop lid
- 2 or 3 small plants
- a few handfuls of gravel
- potting soil
- a stick

1. Put a handful or two of gravel in the jar. Shake the jar gently to get an even covering of gravel.

2. Water the potting soil well, then add a layer on top of the gravel. Make sure the soil is deep enough to cover the roots of the plants.

3. Place the plants in the jar, and gently press the roots into the soil with the stick.

4. Screw the lid back on the jar tightly. Find a light place to keep your garden, but keep it out of direct sunlight. The jar will get too hot inside if it is in bright sun.

5. Observe your garden over time. Don't be tempted to open the bottle to water the garden. You shouldn't need to. Can you see why you don't have to? Your bottle garden should stay healthy for a long time, perhaps several months.

THE WATER CYCLE

Water is just as crucial to the living world as oxygen; without it we couldn't survive. Water moves through the environment in a never-ending cycle known as the water, or hydrological, cycle. Water is continually entering the earth's atmosphere as water vapor, either by evaporating from the land and the surface of the sea or from the leaves of plants. It then forms clouds that will eventually deposit the water elsewhere on the land or sea as rain, snow, or hail. (The bottle environment project on page 11 shows a miniature water cycle in action.)

In many parts of the world, water is a scarce and valuable resource. People's lives depend on having a supply of clean, fresh water.

The hydrological cycle plays an important part in the world's climate systems. The amount of water that is available in a region helps determine the types of plants that grow there. Half the energy that falls on Earth from the sun powers the process of evaporation. Most water evaporates from the hotter regions around the equator, where it forms massive clouds. In the dry, cold polar regions, however, very little water evaporates—the Antarctic is a frozen desert.

Unless there is a shortage, we take water for granted. We use vast amounts of water for drinking and cleaning and in our factories. It takes more than 100,000 gallons (500,000 l) of water to make a car! Growing populations mean agriculture and industry have to expand to provide the food and goods that people need. This increase in demand puts great pressure on our water supplies. Domestic, agricultural, and industrial use of fresh water leaves it polluted. The water has to be specially treated to remove bacteria, chemicals, and other pollutants before it is fit for use again.

DID YOU KNOW?

About 20 percent of the world's fresh water is contained in Lake Baikal in eastern Siberia. It is 5,712 ft. (1,741 m) deep, 385 mi. (620 km) long, and 20–46 mi. (32–74 km) wide.

CLEAN WATER

1. Collect a large pitcherful of pond water, or if you prefer, you can make your own dirty water instead. Collect some soil, leaf litter, twigs, or grass and add to a pitcher of tap water. Mix the ingredients to make the water muddy.

2. Wash the flowerpot and leave it to dry. Then line the inside with filter paper.

3. Put the flowerpot in the dish and fill it one-third full of charcoal. Fill the next third of the pot with the rinsed sand. Use the washed gravel to fill the rest of the pot.

4. Fill a glass jar with pond water—it will be used for comparison later. Hold the sieve over the flowerpot and pour the rest of the pond water from the pitcher in a slow, steady stream. The pond water will collect in the dish under the flowerpot. What happened to it as it traveled through the flowerpot?

MATERIALS

- some pond water, the dirtier the better!
- a large pitcher
- a clay flowerpot
- a large dish
- filter paper
- some broken charcoal
- some rinsed sand
- some washed gravel
- a fine sieve
- 2 glass jars

WARNING!

- Never go near open water alone—it can be dangerous. Always make sure you are accompanied by an adult.

5. Pour the pond water from the dish into the second glass jar. Compare it with the first jar of pond water. Can you see a difference? Don't drink the water! There are still many invisible micro-organisms that your filtering didn't remove.

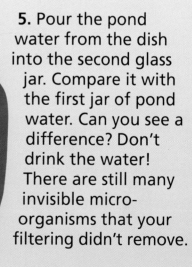

PLANT PUMPS

Plants play an important role in the water cycle. Broad leaves can catch rain before it falls to the ground, allowing it to evaporate back into the atmosphere rather than running off into the soil. Plants also take up water from the soil through their roots and lose it back to the atmosphere through their leaves. This loss of water from the plant is called transpiration. Transpiration is essential to the plant, as the constant stream of water flowing from roots to leaves carries nutrients to all parts of the plant. The amount of water taken up varies from plant to plant. Broad-leaved plants lose most, but even a single corn plant can transpire 54 gal. (245 l) of water in the course of its growing season. You can see why farmers are concerned when droughts threaten their crops!

The loss of trees in large numbers through deforestation can have a crucial effect on a region's climate. Tropical rain forest trees pump huge quantities of water back into the atmosphere. If these trees are cut down, the rainwater will run off into streams and rivers instead of going back into the air. This means that the air is drier, and less rain will fall elsewhere.

PLANT PUMPS

How much water does a plant lose to the atmosphere in a day? This project will help you find out. You need to use two potted plants of the same size and type—nonflowering, broad-leaved plants work best.

1. Make sure both plants are well and evenly watered. Cover one plant completely, pot and all, in a plastic bag and seal the bag tightly.

2. Put the second plant pot in a bag so that the soil is covered but the plant is not. Spread a little petroleum jelly around the neck of the bag to get a good airtight seal. Seal the bag tightly using a tie, but without damaging the plant stem.

3. Weigh both plants and write down the results.

4. Weigh the plants every day for a week, keeping track of the results. Which plant is lightest at the end of the time?

MATERIALS
- 2 potted plants
- 2 large transparent plastic bags
- 2 plant ties
- a set of scales
- petroleum jelly
- a notepad and pen

Rain forest trees pump huge quantities of water back into the atmosphere. Half the rainfall in some forests comes from water that has been cycled through the trees.

You might also like to try placing a plastic bag over a suitably sized leafy tree branch. Make sure that the neck of the bag is tightly closed, using a plant tie to secure it. Leave it for a day to see how much water collects inside the bag.

THE NITROGEN CYCLE

Other elements besides carbon and oxygen are important to living things. Among these are nitrogen, which is essential for making proteins, the chemicals that carry out a number of vital tasks in living things; chlorophyll, the chemical in plants that captures the energy for photosynthesis; and DNA, the chemical in cells that controls their functions and transmits characteristics from one generation to the next.

Nitrogen moves through the environment in a natural cycle. Plants absorb nitrogen compounds from the soil and use them to make proteins. Animals eat the plants and convert the plant protein into animal protein. When an animal dies, bacteria and other organisms break down its body, converting the proteins into nitrogen compounds that can be used by plants again.

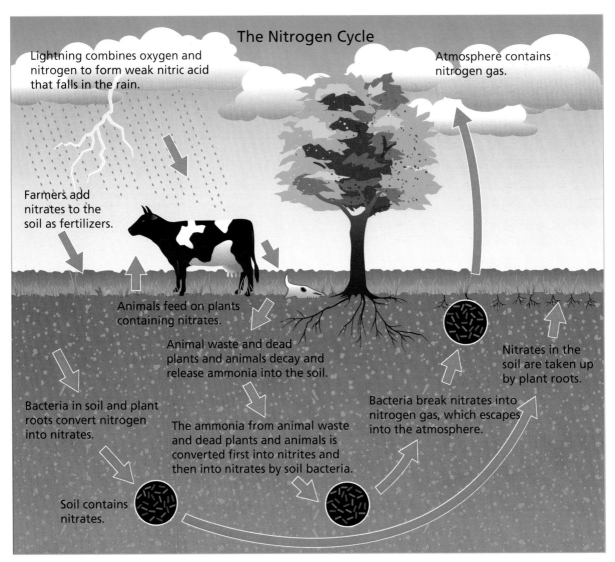

The Nitrogen Cycle

Lightning combines oxygen and nitrogen to form weak nitric acid that falls in the rain.

Atmosphere contains nitrogen gas.

Farmers add nitrates to the soil as fertilizers.

Animals feed on plants containing nitrates.

Animal waste and dead plants and animals decay and release ammonia into the soil.

Nitrates in the soil are taken up by plant roots.

Bacteria in soil and plant roots convert nitrogen into nitrates.

The ammonia from animal waste and dead plants and animals is converted first into nitrites and then into nitrates by soil bacteria.

Bacteria break nitrates into nitrogen gas, which escapes into the atmosphere.

Soil contains nitrates.

NITROGEN AND GROWTH

MATERIALS

- a package of lima bean seeds
- moist sand from a garden center
- potting soil
- 2 seed trays
- a garden trowel
- a plant spray
- chemical fertilizer

Plants need nutrients such as nitrogen to grow and stay healthy. This project compares the development of plants grown in poor soil (soil lacking in nitrogen) with plants grown in rich soil (soil rich in nitrogen).

1. Fill a seed tray with potting soil and place between eight and ten seeds in the tray. The seeds should be evenly spaced and pressed deep into the soil so that they are well covered.

2. Water the soil well and place the tray in a warm, light place. Check the tray every day to make sure the soil is kept moist.

3. After a few days the seeds will sprout into seedlings. When the seedlings are about 1 in. (2.5 cm) tall, divide them into two groups. One group should remain in the seed tray with the compost. The second group should be grown in a seed tray with the moist sand. Make sure that all other conditions, such as light, temperature, and water, are the same for both.

4. Record how your seedlings grow over a few weeks. At first, the seedlings grown on the sand are using nutrients stored in the seed. Once this is used up, what is the effect on the seedlings' development? Do you see any difference between the two groups?

5. Repeat the project, but this time add a pinch of fertilizer to the sand before planting the seedlings. Does the fertilizer affect their development?

FOOD CHAINS AND WEBS

A food chain is a series of organisms, each of which is eaten by the next. Green plants are the first link in a food chain because they use the sun's energy to make their own food by photosynthesis. Ecologists call green plants producers. Animals cannot make their own food—they have to eat plants or other animals. For this reason they are called consumers. A food chain shows how producers and consumers are linked.

Bald eagles, top predators, are at the end of their food chain. However, they are close to extinction because of the damage to their food chain caused by pollution.

A food web is a complex network of food chains involving many species eating different kinds of food. Often the same animals will appear in different chains within the web. For example, earthworms may be preyed on by shrews and songbirds, both of which may be eaten by owls.

A food chain

The caterpillar eats the plant and converts it into caterpillar tissue. The caterpillar is a primary consumer.

The bird eats the caterpillar and converts it into bird tissue. The bird is a secondary consumer.

The cat eats the bird and converts it into cat tissue. The cat is a tertiary consumer. When it dies, bacteria break down its body into nitrates that are released into the soil to be reused by plants. Carbon dioxide and water are also produced by decomposition.

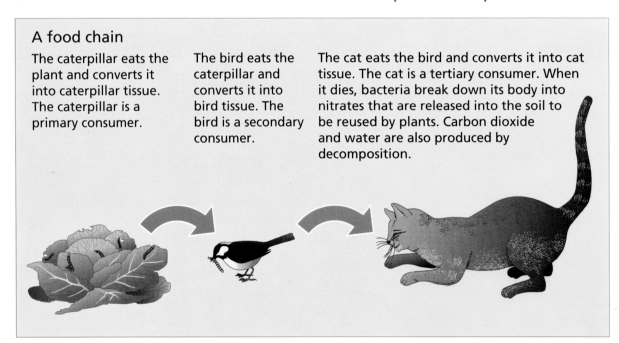

A FOOD WEB MOBILE

1. Choose a bird, such as a hawk or an owl, to be your top predator. (You can attach everything else to their outspread wings.) Find out what smaller birds and mammals the hawk eats. Then find out what the birds and mammals eat, so you have at least three different food chains.

2. Draw the plants and animals yourself or photocopy or trace pictures from books or magazines.

3. Glue each picture onto a separate piece of colored cardboard. Attach the picture of the top predator to the clothes hanger with tape or modeling clay.

4. Make some small holes along the bottom of the top predator—one for each of the animals in the next layer of each food chain. Hang the pictures under the top predator with equal lengths of string. You might need to stick small lumps of modeling clay to the backs of the pictures to balance them.

5. Repeat the process to complete each food chain. Use tape and string to link the predators that appear in different chains within the web.

Try making your mobile the other way up. Have a strip of plants at the top with everything else hanging below so your top predator is farthest away from the plant strip. What would happen if you broke one of the links in the web?

MATERIALS
- a clothes hanger
- stiff, colored cardboard
- scissors
- colored string
- tape
- colored pens or pencils
- modeling clay
- glue

EFFICIENT EATING

There is inevitably a loss of energy within a food chain. A pound of leaves will not produce a pound of caterpillars, for example. Perhaps only 10 percent of the energy the plant captured from the sun will be stored in the caterpillar's tissue. Not all of the plant is consumed and digested, so some energy is lost in the waste material. More energy is converted into heat by the caterpillar's respiration. The caterpillar uses energy crawling from leaf to leaf.

To account for this energy loss, ecologists have a third way of looking at feeding relationships in addition to chains and webs. This is known as an energy pyramid. The diagram below shows how an energy pyramid works.

An energy pyramid rarely has more than five levels. The fewer the levels, the more efficient an energy pyramid is, as less energy is needed to support the top level consumers. It is cheaper for people to eat grain themselves than to use the grain to feed cattle and eat meat. This partly explains why people in underdeveloped and overcrowded countries tend to eat little meat. More people can be fed from an area where crops are grown than if the same area is used to graze animals.

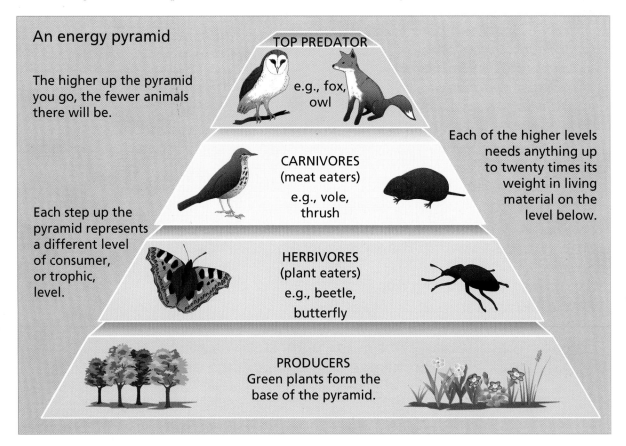

An energy pyramid

The higher up the pyramid you go, the fewer animals there will be.

Each step up the pyramid represents a different level of consumer, or trophic, level.

TOP PREDATOR
e.g., fox, owl

Each of the higher levels needs anything up to twenty times its weight in living material on the level below.

CARNIVORES
(meat eaters)
e.g., vole, thrush

HERBIVORES
(plant eaters)
e.g., beetle, butterfly

PRODUCERS
Green plants form the base of the pyramid.

RELEASING FOOD ENERGY

1. Carefully push the eye of the needle into the cork, then press the peanut onto the pointed end. Don't press too hard or you might break the nut.

2. Use the can opener to remove both ends of the large can. Ask an adult to punch two holes in the small can, near the top and exactly opposite each other.

3. Thread the skewer through the holes in the small can. Pour the cup of water into the small can and let it sit for an hour to come to room temperature. Put the thermometer into the water and record the temperature.

4. Put the peanut and cork on the metal tray. Then ask an adult to set fire to the peanut, using the matches. As soon as the peanut is lit, place the large can over it and hang the small can inside the large one, using the skewer.

5. When the nut has burned out, stir the water with the thermometer and measure the temperature again. What has happened to the energy in the nut? Repeat the experiment, using different varieties of nuts to see which kind releases the most energy.

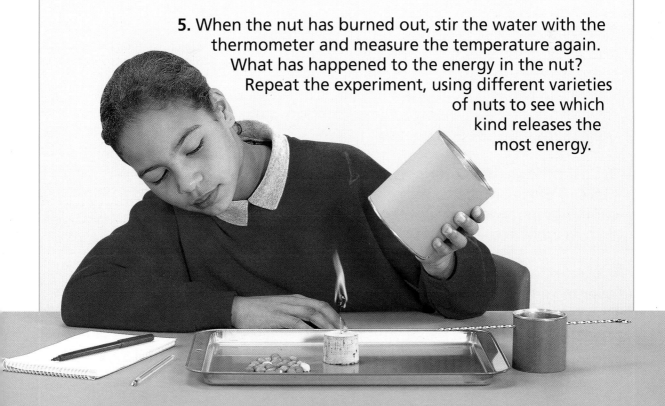

DECOMPOSERS

Decomposers are the environmental cleanup squad. They are a crucial part of the environment, for they deal with the waste material and, eventually, the dead bodies of other organisms. Decomposers are consumers, but they are different from other consumers in that they break down the material they consume into the inorganic nutrients that the producers need. These nutrients are released into the soil, water, and air, to be used again.

The decomposers-in-chief are fungi and bacteria. There are more bacteria than any other kind of living organism. Billions of them inhabit every handful of fertile soil. Decomposers can be found almost everywhere, even inside your body! Bacteria living in your intestines convert partially digested food into nutrients that your body can use. Without them more of the food you eat would simply pass through your body as waste.

MAKING COMPOST

1. Ask your family to collect the kitchen waste that would usually be thrown away during a day, for example, eggshells, teabags, coffee grounds, potato peelings, and other uncooked vegetable waste.

2. After a day or so you should have collected enough kitchen waste to start making your compost. Fill the bottom of the large container with a layer of waste, about 4 to 6 in. (10 to 15 cm) deep. Don't add plants to your compost as their seeds may not decompose.

3. Cover the waste material with about 1 in. (2.5 cm) of soil. Make sure that your soil contains plenty of worms and other creatures such as woodlice, ants, and millipedes.

4. Continue to build up the layers with a thin layer of soil between each layer of compost. Don't pack the layers too tightly. It is important that air circulate through the compost. Make your top layer a layer of soil.

MATERIALS
- kitchen waste
- a container with a lid (to store your kitchen waste in)
- grass cuttings
- a large container with a rainproof lid
- a spade
- soil
- chemical fertilizer or starter compost with nitrogen

WARNING!
- Don't put weeds in your compost! Unless the inside of the compost gets hot enough to kill them, the weed seeds can survive the composting process.

Larger organisms such as earthworms and maggots are also classed as decomposers, or detritivores. They feed on material, called detritus, produced by the decomposition of animals and plants. These decomposers partially break down the organic matter. The fungi and bacteria finish the process, reducing the matter further to release the nutrients locked up in it.

Fungi are some of the main agents of decomposition in the natural world. They help break down all kinds of organic material, releasing chemicals that can be recycled.

5. Add some fertilizer or starter compost to your compost; both contain nitrogen that will help your compost to work properly. Grass cuttings are rich in nitrogen, too, but fertilizer will get your compost working faster.

6. Bacteria, fungi, earthworms, and other organisms will all get to work on your compost. You won't be able to see the bacteria, but you will know they are at work. The inside of your compost will get hot—this heat is produced by the bacteria. The compost should reach its top temperature in about two to three weeks.

In about three months your compost will be ready to use in the garden. Adding compost to flowerbeds and vegetable patches will help the plants grow.

CLIMATE

The climate of an area is the average weather conditions, such as temperature, rainfall, humidity, amount of sunlight, and wind speeds found there over time. The driving force of the world's climate systems is energy received from the sun.

More solar energy is received in the regions around the equator, the imaginary line around the middle of the earth, than at the poles, so the climate is hot at the equator and cool at the poles. Warm air rises from the equatorial regions and flows out to the poles, where it cools and sinks, flowing back to the equator again. If it were not for the transportation of heat from the equator to the poles, most of the earth's surface would be uninhabitable because it would be either too hot or too cold.

The two most important climatic factors in determining the kinds of plants and animals found in an area are temperature and rainfall. Tropical rain forests are found in areas with high temperatures and lots of rain. Many plants grow there, providing a rich and varied environment for animals. Only a few plants and animals are adapted to live in the dry conditions of hot deserts, however.

Most plants and animals would be unable to survive in the harsh conditions of a desert, with its extremes of hot and cold.

MINIATURE CLIMATES

In this experiment you can try growing one type of seed in a variety of different environments and try to determine which one suits it best.

MATERIALS
- a package of cress seeds
- 4 small plastic cups
- cotton or tissue paper
- a notepad and pencil
- a ruler

1. Fill three of your cups with loosely packed, wet tissue paper or cotton. Scatter some seeds on the top of each cup.

2. Place one of the cups in a warm, light place. Remember to sprinkle it with water every day. This is your warm, damp climate zone.

3. Put the second cup in the refrigerator. Take it out each day to give it a little water. This is the cold climate zone.

4. Put the third cup in the freezer. This can represent Arctic conditions.

5. Fill the fourth cup with dry cotton or tissue paper. Sprinkle some seeds on the top and put it where it will get as much direct sunlight as possible. Do not give it any water. This is the hot, dry climate zone.

6. Observe your seeds over a week or so. Measure them daily and keep note of how they develop. Which cups do best? Do any of your seeds not grow at all? What happens to the seeds in the freezer if you let them defrost? From the results of your experiment can you say which factor is most important to the seeds—light, warmth, or water, or a combination of all three?

Are the second and third "climates" fair tests? If not, why not?

HABITATS

The place where an organism lives, its local environment, is called its habitat. This is where it will find most of what it needs to survive and reproduce.

A habitat can be as enormous as a rain forest or an ocean. Each major habitat can be divided into many, perhaps thousands, of smaller habitats.

Coral reefs are one of the richest of the earth's habitats. They are home to a huge and diverse range of fish species.

WOOD LOUSE WORLD

1. Ask an adult to make some holes in the lids of your collecting jars so the wood lice can breathe.

2. Collect between 10 and 20 wood lice. A good place to look for wood lice is under plant pots, stones, and logs in your yard or in the park. Pick up the wood lice very gently with the paintbrush so they won't be injured.

MATERIALS
- 10 to 20 wood lice
- a large plastic tray
- a spray bottle
- a notepad and pencil
- a garden trowel
- a piece of cardboard or old cloth to cover part of the tray
- soil
- some jars with lids
- a fine paintbrush
- a hammer and nail (for making holes in your jar lids)

3. Put a layer of soil in the tray. Don't fill the tray to the top or the wood lice will escape!

4. Use the spray bottle to dampen the soil in one half of the tray. Put the wood lice in the tray and let them wander freely. You might need to tap the tray every few minutes to keep the wood lice moving.

The water world covers a range of habitats, from the depths of the oceans to freshwater ponds, and a huge variety of creatures have evolved to live in all these habitats. Habitats can change over a short distance—think of the seashore, where there can be underwater, tidal, and dry land zones all within a short distance.

A very precisely defined habitat is called a microhabitat. A microhabitat can be under a stone where an insect lives or a pool of water in a tree hollow. A single plant in a forest can have beetles living in its stem, caterpillars on its leaves, and fungus growing on its roots. Each part of the plant is a microhabitat for different organisms.

Every habitat has its own set of environmental conditions, and most will be home to a wide variety of animals and plants. The organisms that live there will be adapted, or suited, to those conditions. Many organisms can live only in a single well-defined habitat because they are so closely adapted to it. A fish, for example, would suffocate if it were taken onto land because its gills are not adapted for breathing air.

5. Every 15 minutes count the number of wood lice in each half of the tray. If the damp half seems to be drying out, spray it again. After a few counts add up your results. Divide the total for each half, wet or dry, by the number of counts you made. In which half of the tray did you find most wood lice on average?

6. Try the experiment again but under different conditions. This time dampen all of the soil but cover half of the tray with an old cloth or some cardboard. Where do you find most wood lice now—in the light or in the dark?

7. When the experiment is over, take your wood lice back to where you found them and let them go. The places in which you found your wood lice should have given you an idea of the conditions they like. Did your experiments back this up?

A JOB FOR LIFE

The place occupied by an organism in its habitat is called its niche. This describes the way in which the organism fits into its environment and how it relates to all the other living things that share its habitat. It also describes the organism's relationships with the nonliving parts of its environment. If you think of an organism's habitat as its home, then perhaps you might consider its niche as its job, what it does within its habitat.

Ecologists believe that no two species can occupy exactly the same niche. If they did there would inevitably be competition between them. One species would drive the other species to extinction.

Some organisms are suited to a broad range of conditions and so have very wide niches. Think of humans, who have used their intelligence and adaptability to make homes all over the world in conditions ranging from the cold of the Arctic to the heat of the tropical rain forests. Other organisms are so highly adapted to their environment that they need to have very specific conditions for their survival. For example, fish that have adapted to the extreme pressure and cold of the

The flower, as a source of food, is part of the insect's niche. The insect, as a pollinator, is part of the flower's niche.

deep ocean will die if they are brought nearer the surface.

OBSERVATION STATIONS

MATERIALS

- a few jars or clean yogurt containers
- some large, flat stones
- a few small pebbles
- a garden trowel
- an insect field guide
- soil and leaf litter to put in your jars

1. Plan where you are going to put your jars. Try to place each one in a different habitat from the next. If you live near a park or some woodland you might put the first jar under some ground weeds, the second one under a deciduous tree, the third one under a conifer tree, and the last one a short distance away under some grass.

2. Use the trowel to dig a hole just big enough for your jar. The hole should be deep enough so that the top of the jar doesn't stand above the surface of the ground. Place your jar upright in the hole.

3. Put some soil and leaf litter in the jar to attract the animals (and provide them with some food and shelter until you come to release them!). Put a few pebbles around the jar and place a large, flat stone over it, balanced on the pebbles. This will prevent your catch from drowning if it rains.

4. Leave the jars overnight. Did you find different animals in each one? Are some animals found in all your jars? Carry out the experiment over several days, checking the jars and freeing the captured creatures each morning. Use the field guide to try and identify your catch.

There may be fewer animals in your jars by morning than the number that actually fell in overnight. Why do you think this is?

COMMUNITIES

We often think of people as living in different communities, according to where they live and what they do. Some people live in cities, and some in small towns. There are farming communities and fishing communities. Plants and animals also live in communities. A community is a group of organisms that share a habitat and interact in many ways. The community might be defined by the dominant plant species or by a particular feature of the habitat, such as an oak wood community or a pond community. The community includes everything that lives there. A pond community, for example, means the worms in the mud, the fish in the water, the algae floating on the surface, and everything in between.

A North American pine forest community might include bear, deer, and wolves.

Similar communities can be grouped together into biomes. A biome can be extremely large. It need not be a single area but the basic conditions in each place will be the same. All the world's hot deserts may be thought of as a single biome, for instance. Although great distances of land and ocean separate the Mojave Desert in North America from the Sahara Desert in North Africa, for example, both have high daytime temperatures and low rainfall. In each there are plants and animals that are adapted to those conditions. Other biomes include the Arctic tundra biome and the tropical rain forest biome.

TREE COMMUNITIES

MATERIALS
- a magnifying lens
- an old white sheet
- some jars with lids
- a fine paintbrush
- an insect field guide
- a hammer and nail (for making holes in your jar lids)

1. Ask an adult to make some holes in the lids of your collecting jars so the animals can breathe.

2. Find a suitable tree branch—one that's low enough to reach easily. Place the sheet on the ground under the branch.

3. Shake the branch vigorously, but not so hard that you break it! Your sheet will catch whatever falls from the tree.

4. Look carefully at what you find. A field guide will help you sort your specimens. Put a few animals of different types into your collecting jars for a closer look. Use the paintbrush gently to pick up the smaller ones. Be wary about putting different animals in the same jar in case one eats the other!

5. Repeat the project with a different type of tree. Do you find the same animals? You won't be able to find all of the tree animals in this way; some you won't dislodge from the branch and others will simply fly away! However, if you look carefully at your catch you will begin to get some idea of the rich community supported by a tree.

POPULATIONS

No living thing exists in isolation from others of its kind. Even a normally solitary animal, such as a tiger, must meet another member of its species to reproduce. A group of organisms of the same species living within a particular area is called a population.

No population stays the same. In any community, human or otherwise, individuals are born and die. If a population has a higher number of births in one year than it has deaths, then that population will increase. Given ideal conditions, a population can increase dramatically. If all its offspring survived, a single aphid could give rise to 600 billion offspring in a single season!

Populations are prevented from increasing beyond a certain level by a number of factors. Individuals compete with each other for food and living

CAPTURE RECAPTURE

Here is a simple method for estimating the population of an animal species.

You will need to set up your observation stations again, as you did on page 29. This time, however, you should be on the lookout for a particular creature that is easy for you to identify. A large species of beetle would be ideal. You may have to consult a field guide for your locality.

as you did on page 29

MATERIALS
- 4 or 5 jars
- a fine paintbrush
- some nontoxic paint
- an insect field guide
- a notebook and pencil
- a lid from a jar

1. Choose an area to set up your observation stations. You might want to survey the beetle population in your yard, perhaps, or in a local park or woodland. Leave the jars in place overnight.

2. Return to your jars in the morning and take a look inside. Select a particular type of beetle and mark each one with a drop of paint on its back.

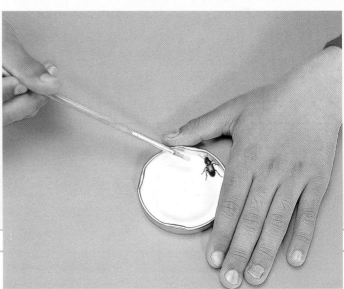

space. Other species might compete for the same food resource. Disease can spread rapidly through an overcrowded population, while predators help to keep numbers down.

Sometimes it is a difficult task to count the number of individuals in a population. Imagine trying to count the number of aphids on a rosebush, for example! However, as the project below shows, there is a method for counting small animal populations that you can try for yourself.

These king penguins live together in colonies of many thousands, huddling together to keep warm.

3. Release your catch back into their habitat and give them a chance to mix with the rest of the beetles. You can leave your jars in position but cover them so nothing can fall in. After a couple of days reset the jars as before.

4. Now examine your second catch. Count all the beetles you have captured this time and count the number that have a mark from the first capture.

5. Calculate the total population of beetles in your area like this. Multiply the number of beetles in the first capture by the number of beetles in the second capture and divide the answer by the number of marked beetles in the second capture. This will give you the population.

$$\frac{n_1 \times n_2}{n_m} = \text{population}$$

You can use this technique to survey populations in different areas and at different times.

ECOSYSTEMS

The interlinking of the species in a community, combined with their relationships with their physical environment, makes up an ecosystem. The difference between an ecosystem and a biome is that the nonliving part of the environment is included in the ecosystem.

Ecosystems are usually finely balanced and stable, with resources constantly being recycled. Food chains are the pathways through which nutrients pass between the organisms in the ecosystem. Removing a single species may have a disastrous effect on the ecosystem as a whole. For example, if a predator is wiped out, the population of the animal it preys on can grow unchecked. The result of this might be overgrazing, leading to the loss of vital plant species and the eventual destruction of the ecosystem.

An ecosystem may consist of several linked habitats. A river habitat may be linked to a woodland habitat by the animals that come to hunt and drink there. Ecosystems are in turn linked to other ecosystems—the whole planet Earth could be considered as one hugely complex ecosystem.

MAKE AN ECOSYSTEM

Making a minipond is a good way to observe plants and animals interacting. You can buy most of these materials from an aquarium supply shop, or if you know someone who has a pond, you could borrow the materials from them instead.

1. Choose a place for your tank away from direct sunlight. If the water gets too warm the animals will die. Put the gravel in the bottom of the tank, sloping it from the back to the front so that it is about twice as deep at the back. There should be about 1 in. (2.5 cm) of gravel at the front.

MATERIALS

- an aquarium tank
- a bag of clean gravel
- a few well-scrubbed stones
- 3 to 4 water weeds
- some floating plants, such as duckweed
- a selection of pond animals
- 1 cup (200 ml) of pond mud
- a net for collecting pond animals
- a pitcher
- a ruler
- a pond guide
- some containers with lids for collecting pond animals
- a notebook and pencil

2. Wash your water plants and remove any dead leaves. Push the stems of the plants gently into the gravel and anchor them in position with the stones. Don't put in too many plants or you might suffocate your animals.

3. Using the pitcher, pour the tap water gently into the tank until it's about three-fourths full. Try not to disturb the gravel and plants.

4. Carefully add about 1 cup (200 ml) of pond mud to the tank. This may contain eggs or larvae that will emerge later. Leave the tank for a day or two to settle.

5. Collect as many different pond animals as you can find. Use a pond guide to help identify the animals.

6. Introduce the animals to the tank. Watch them carefully over time and keep a record of what goes on in your minipond. Can you see what each animal eats? Have you created a balanced ecosystem, and if not, what can you do to balance it? For example, what would happen if you removed most of the predators from the tank? Can you draw a food web for your minipond?

If you take care of your minipond, it will go on giving you pleasure for a long time. When you have finished your observations return any animals you took from the wild back to their natural habitat.

WARNING!

● Never go near open water alone—it can be dangerous. Always make sure you are accompanied by an adult.

WASTE NOT, WANT NOT

As we have seen, very little in the natural world is wasted. Eventually, almost everything is broken down and recycled. How does this compare to the way humans behave? Much of the trash we produce, such as plastic for example, is not naturally recyclable—the natural decomposers cannot deal with it. For instance, if you buried a plastic bag in the ground and dug it up five years later you would find the bag still intact, just as you left it.

Our waste pollutes the landscape, the water supply, and the atmosphere. However, we can learn to recycle a great deal of this material ourselves. Cardboard and paper can be de-inked and pulped to make new paper. Waste glass can be added to the mix in a furnace when new glass is being made. In fact, if waste glass is added, the new glass can be made at lower furnace temperatures so this also saves some energy.

Much of our waste is simply dumped in vast landfill sites. A lot of the material here might have been recycled.

Aluminum is a very common metal. We use it to make all kinds of goods from soft drink cans to parts for cars and airplanes. Producing aluminum is an expensive and environmentally damaging process. Much of the bauxite from which aluminum is extracted is mined from tropical forest regions. Melting down an aluminum can for reuse takes just 5 percent of the energy used to make a new one.

Metals and fossil fuels are continually being extracted from the earth, yet they exist only in limited amounts. They are nonrenewable resources: resources that cannot be replaced once they have been used up by human activity. Eventually there will be no oil left to make the fuel we need to run our cars, planes, and other mechanized transportation. What will we do then?

A RECYCLING SCULPTURE

1. Collect as many different objects as you can—such as egg cartons, plastic bottles, cans, and paper and food packaging.

2. Build a sculpture out of the objects you have collected.

MATERIALS
- items of reusable household waste
- glue
- scissors

Use your imagination to make your sculpture as colorful and creative as you like!

PEST CONTROL

We usually call any organism a pest if it harms us or our food plants or domestic animals. Because we grow vast areas of crops and keep large herds of animals, it is inevitable that these concentrations of food will attract other species, too. Often farmers try to control the pests with chemicals. These chemicals are called pesticides and include insecticides for insect control, herbicides for weed control, fungicides for controlling fungal pests like molds and mildew, and poisons for rats and mice.

The great danger in using pesticides is that beneficial insects like bees may be killed along with the pests. Animals higher up the food chain can also be affected if they eat sprayed insects. Since the predator will consume several poisoned insects, it will get a bigger dose of the pesticide. Several types of pesticides are thought to cause cancer in humans, too.

One alternative to the chemical control of pests is to use natural predators instead. This is called biological control. For example, entomologists discovered that certain parasites attack and destroy several species of moths that attack cabbages. Breeding these parasites and releasing them in cabbage fields brings about a sharp decline in the pests.

BIOLOGICAL CONTROL

Aphids are common garden pests, sucking juices from plants, weakening them, and spreading diseases. Ladybugs, both adults and their larvae, are predators of aphids.

1. Ask an adult to make some holes in the lid of your container so the ladybugs can breathe.

2. Find a small plant, in a garden or elsewhere, that is infested with aphids. Carefully dig it up, making sure not to disturb the aphids too much.

3. Replant it in the pot, using soil from where you found the plant. Now collect a number of ladybugs. You should find lots where the aphids are! Use the paintbrush to pick them up and put them in the container.

MATERIALS
- an aquarium tank with a fine mesh top
- a plant infested by aphids
- a number of ladybugs
- a flowerpot
- a fine paintbrush
- a container with a lid
- a garden trowel
- a hammer and nail (for making holes in your container lid)

Another method is to sterilize male insects by exposing them to radiation. When they are released, the sterile males mate with the females, which then lay infertile eggs from which no young will hatch.

Poison buildup in a food chain

The farmer sprays the crops with pesticide, which leaves a small amount of poison on each seed and insect.

Mice eat the seeds and insects. The pesticide on each seed and insect builds up inside each mouse.

The owl consumes several mice and gets an even larger dose of pesticide.

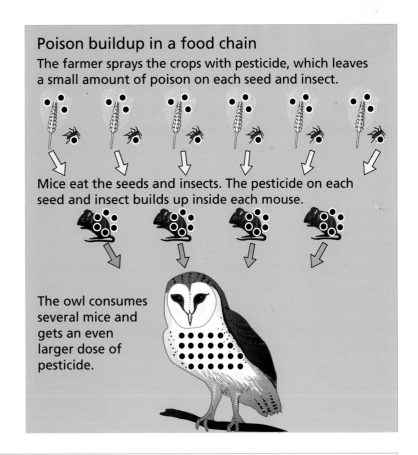

4. Put the plant in the tank and then release the ladybugs into the tank. Put the fine mesh over the tank to keep the ladybugs from escaping.

5. Observe the ladybugs and aphids closely over the next few days. Do the ladybugs keep the aphid numbers in check or do the aphid numbers increase? What would happen if you added more ladybugs or took some out? What key differences do you see in ladybug and aphid behavior?

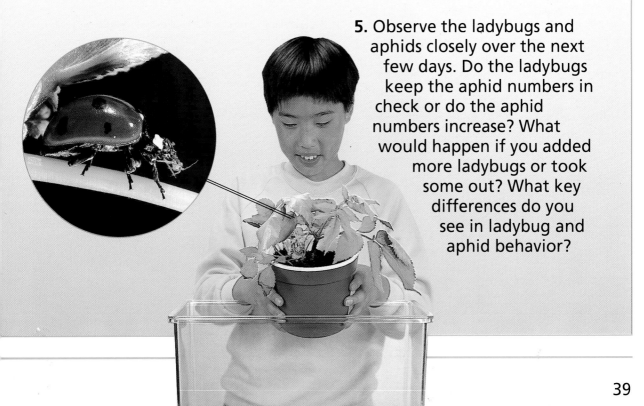

FERTILIZERS

On pages 16 and 17 we looked at the nitrogen cycle. When farmers harvest their crops they disrupt the nutrients in the cycle by taking away material that would normally be recycled by the decomposers in the soil. They remove nutrients from the ecosystem, causing it to become unbalanced. If this continues, the soil eventually becomes poor in nutrients and unable to sustain a decent crop. The most certain way of replacing the lost nutrients is to add fertilizers to the soil. Fertilizers can be organic, for example farmyard manure, which is rich in nitrogen, or inorganic, artificial fertilizers, which are produced in a factory.

The fertilizers that farmers put on their fields can cause problems if they get into the surrounding environment. Nitrogen and phosphorus, found in fertilizers, are essential for the chemical reactions involved in photosynthesis. However, plants need only a very small amount and often too much is applied to fields. Rain washes the excess out of the fields and into the water supply. If you have ever seen a river choked with

Huge quantities of fertilizers are used to make agricultural land more productive. They replace the nutrients lost from the soil when crops are harvested.

weeds or a pond that looks like pea soup you have seen the effects of fertilizer runoff.

Excess phosphate and nitrate cause the algae in a pond to increase enormously. This artificial enrichment of the water is called eutrophication. Algae use up oxygen in the water as they respire. When they die, decomposing bacteria deplete the oxygen in the pond. Eventually the other organisms in the pond suffocate and die.

Nitrates in the water supply can also become a hazard to humans. Nitrates are converted into nitrites in the stomachs of very young babies. When the nitrites get into the bloodstream, they interfere with the ability of the blood to carry oxygen around the body. This can result in what is called blue-baby syndrome, which can be fatal. Links between nitrates in water and stomach cancers in adults have also been suggested, but this has not been proven.

EUTROPHICATION

The nitrogen and growth project on page 17 showed how chemical fertilizer can benefit the soil. In the experiment below you can investigate one of the hazards of fertilizer use.

MATERIALS
- 2 large jars of pond water
- chemical fertilizer

WARNING!
- Never go near open water alone—it can be dangerous. Always make sure you are accompanied by an adult.

1. Collect two jars of water from a healthy pond (a pond that is free from eutrophication). Alternatively, you can use some pond water from your minipond. Each of your pond samples will contain some algae.

2. Add a pinch of fertilizer to one of the jars. Observe the jars over a few days. Do you see a marked difference in the amount of algae that grows in the jar that contains the fertilizer? This is what happens when ponds are contaminated by fertilizer from farms.

GLOBAL THREATS

Humans pose perhaps the biggest threat to the global environment through the huge amounts of chemicals that are pumped directly into the atmosphere from factories, power plants, and car exhausts. Chlorofluorocarbons (CFCs), used as aerosol propellants and in refrigerators, cause the breakdown of ozone, a gas that forms a protective layer in the atmosphere by absorbing harmful ultraviolet radiation from the sun. Increases in the amounts of ultraviolet radiation reaching the earth from the sun could damage crops and ecosystems and cause skin cancer and cataracts in humans. International agreements call for a ban on the production of CFCs by the year 2000.

When fossil fuels and firewood are burned most of the carbon in the fuel combines with oxygen to form carbon dioxide. Some unburned carbon remains in the atmosphere as tiny particles that can block out sunlight, reducing the light available for photosynthesis. Approximately

MEASURING AIR POLLUTION

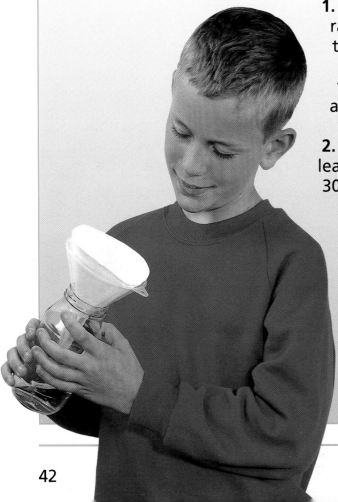

MATERIALS
- a jar
- a funnel
- some filter paper
- a magnifying lens

1. Wait for a rainy day. Place the funnel, lined with the filter paper, in a clean jar.

2. Take your apparatus outside and leave it in a safe place for at least 30 minutes.

3. Bring the apparatus inside and wait for the filter paper to dry out.

4. Use the magnifying lens to examine the dirt that has collected on the filter paper. Can you identify the particles of carbon that have come down with the rain?

5 billion tons of carbon dioxide are released into the atmosphere every year by human activities. Many environmentalists believe the increasing levels of carbon dioxide will lead to an overall warming of the planet and catastrophic climate changes.

The atmosphere contains sulfur dioxide from volcanoes and other natural sources. The sulfur dioxide combines with water vapor to become sulfuric acid in rainwater. The burning of fuels doubles the amount of sulfur dioxide in the atmosphere and raises the acidity to dangerous levels. Burning of fuels also releases nitrogen oxides into the atmosphere, forming nitric acid in rainwater. Acid rain can damage buildings, remove nutrients from the soil, destroy forests, and kill the fish and plant life in ponds.

AIR POLLUTION SURVEY

1. Measure and mark 1 in. (2.5 cm) in from the edges of each piece of cardboard. Use the marks to draw a smaller square inside the large one.

2. Cut out the inner square of each piece of cardboard to make a frame.

3. Peel the backing off the self-adhesive plastic and place the frames on the sticky side of the plastic.

4. Leave the frames with the sticky side up in different places outside. Try to vary the locations as much as possible. It might be a good idea to work with a friend or classmate who lives in a different area from you.

5. After a few days, examine the frames with the magnifying lens and record your results. Is there a difference between town and country or between different parts of your town or area? Where is it dirtiest and where is it cleanest?

MATERIALS

- several pieces of cardboard 6 in. square (15 cm square)
- several pieces of clear, self-adhesive plastic (the same size as your pieces of cardboard)
- scissors
- a ruler
- a pencil
- a magnifying lens
- a notepad and pen

CONSERVATION

There is still a huge amount to discover about the complex interrelationships between the living world and the non-living world. Yet, sad to say, the number of species and ecosystems on the earth is rapidly diminishing. No one knows how many millions of species there are in the world. In a recent study of just 19 tropical forest trees, a researcher found over 750 species of beetles that had never been identified before. Ecologists refer to the great variety of life that exists as biodiversity. The goal of every conservationist is to try to preserve biodiversity as far as possible.

Many species are becoming extinct; many without ever having been named. The destruction of the rain forests, the most species-rich places on Earth, is a tragic loss. Habitats are being destroyed through land clearance and exploitation of resources. Pollution also

MAKING A BIRDBATH

Why not help out some of the living things that share your garden or school athletic fields? Here are two ideas.

MATERIALS
● a garbage can lid
● 4 blocks of wood or old bricks
● a large pitcher of water

1. Choose a site for a birdbath. Make sure it is in the open where the birds will get warning of any approaching cats, and you will get a good view of the birds!

2. Arrange the blocks of wood in a square on the ground and balance the upturned garbage can lid on top.

3. Fill the lid with clean water for the birds to drink and bathe in.

4. Make sure you change the water every week or so.

threatens life. Perhaps 20 percent of the earth's species face extinction over the next 25 to 30 years. That means gone for good—extinction cannot be reversed. Every species lost is a broken link in a food web, a weakening of an ecosystem, and that could have unpredictable consequences for our planet. Humans benefit directly from many species, and there are sound economic reasons for preserving them.

Almost 5,000 different plant species have been used as food. We also get many medicines from chemicals produced by plants and fungi. Plant and animal fibers are used to make cloth. Trees are used for fuel, building material, and paper. Are we willing to change the way we live in order to preserve as rich a variety of habitats and species as possible? It could be up to you.

MAKING A BIRD FEEDER

1. Make two holes opposite each other in the bottom of the bottle.

2. Thread a length of wire through the holes and tie a loop from which to hang your feeder.

3. Ask an adult to help you cut three or four slits in the sides of the bottle. The slits should start about halfway up the bottle and run from top to bottom. Don't make them too big or the nuts will fall out!

4. Push a couple of sticks through one or two slits to give the birds something to perch on. Fill the bottle with nuts, then replace the top. Hang the bottle from a strong branch.

Leave an untidy corner in the yard or school grounds to encourage insects and other small animals. Add an old log and some flat stones for "bug shelters." Let wild plants grow here. Backyards can be refuges for wildlife—every little bit helps!

MATERIALS
- an empty plastic bottle
- a large bag of shelled, unsalted peanuts
- a length of wire or very strong thread
- 2 to 3 sticks of wood
- scissors

GLOSSARY

Aphids Small insects such as greenfly and blackfly that suck plant juices, causing the plant damage.

Atmosphere The layer of gases that surrounds the earth.

Carbon dioxide A gas that is naturally present in the atmosphere. It is produced by animals when they breathe and is used by plants in photosynthesis. It is also given off when carbon-containing compounds such as coal and oil are burned.

Climate The average weather conditions in a specific place over a long time.

Community A collection of plants and animals living within an area.

Consumer An organism that must feed on other organisms to obtain its food. All animals are consumers.

Decomposer An organism that obtains its energy by breaking down dead organisms or plant and animal wastes.

Deforestation The deliberate clearing of a forest by cutting down and burning trees.

Diversity The variety of different species found within an ecosystem.

Ecology The study of relationships between organisms and their natural environment.

Ecosystem A community of living organisms and their relationships with each other and their physical environment.

Entomologists Scientists who study insects.

Environment The surroundings within which an organism lives and that have an influence on it, including all other living things, climate, and physical conditions.

Fossil fuels Fuels, such as coal, petroleum, and natural gas that have been created from the remains of living organisms by the effects of heat and pressure within the earth.

Habitat A place where a plant or animal lives, such as a desert, a pond, or a tree stump.

Hydrological cycle (or water cycle) The constant movement of water through the environment. Water from the land, sea, and plants evaporates into the atmosphere where it forms clouds that will eventually deposit the water back on Earth.

Nutrient cycle The process by which nutrients are constantly recycled around an ecosystem by living and nonliving matter.

Parasite An organism that lives on and feeds off another organism, often destroying it in the process.

Photosynthesis The process in which green plants make food out of water and carbon dioxide using energy from the sun.

Pollution Substances, such as waste chemicals from factories, that dirty or poison the air, land, and water.

Predator An animal that kills another animal for food.

Recycle To reuse a material, often in a different form, to conserve energy and resources.

Respiration The process in which plants and animals break down organic substances to release energy that they can use. Most plants and animals need oxygen for respiration and give off carbon dioxide in the process.

Solar energy Energy from the sun.

Ultraviolet radiation Powerful energy from the sun that is harmful to humans and the environment.

FURTHER INFORMATION

BOOKS

Bonnet, Bob and Dan Keen. *Science Fair Projects: The Environment*. New York: Sterling Publications, 1995.

Gay, Kathlyn. *Saving the Environment: Debating the Costs* (Impact). Danbury, CT: Franklin Watts, 1996.

Hamilton, John. *Eco-Groups: Joining Together to Protect the Environment* (Target Earth). Edina, MN: Abdo & Daughters, 1993.

Simon, Seymour. *Earth Words: A Dictionary of the Environment*. New York: Harpercrest, 1995.

Vancleave, Janice. *Janice Vancleave's Ecology for Every Kid: Easy Activities That Make Learning About the Environment Fun* (Science for Every Kid). New York: John Wiley & Sons, 1995.

Wright, David. *Facts on File Environment Atlas*. New York: Facts on File, 1998.

CD-ROMS

Exploring Land Habitats and *Exploring Water Habitats* (Raintree Steck-Vaughn, 1997)

ANSWERS TO QUESTIONS

Answers to questions posed in the projects.

Page 7 Light is vital for a plant's well-being. Keeping a plant in the dark is like starving it. A plant that has no access to light will have a thin weak stem. The leaves will become yellow and fall off.

Page 9 If the splint flames up again, you have collected oxygen from the plant.

Page 11 Water given off by the plant will condense on the inside of the bottle and trickle down into the soil to be used again.

Page 13 You should find that the water has been filtered by the contents of the flowerpot. The largest bits and pieces in the water will have been trapped by the sieve. The gravel will have trapped fragments missed by the sieve. The sand, charcoal, and filter paper will have trapped progressively smaller particles of debris.

Pages 14–15 You should find that the plant that was exposed weighs less than the plant that was entirely covered. The water lost by the covered plant will have been trapped by the bag, whereas the water lost by the exposed plant will have evaporated into the air.

Page 17 The seedlings cannot obtain any nutrients from the sand. Once their seed store is used up they will become stunted. Although they can make sugars by photosynthesis they cannot make proteins with which to build new plant material. Adding fertilizer provides the nitrogen the plants need to grow.

Page 19 Breaking a link in the web causes the mobile to become unbalanced. Similarly, breaking a link in a real food web, when a plant or animal becomes extinct, can upset the natural balance, with possibly disastrous effects on the other organisms in the web.

Page 21 You will have released the chemical energy in the nut and used it to heat the water.

Page 25 You should find that the seeds in the first pot do best. Most plants need a combination of light, water, and warmth to do well. The seeds that are in the refrigerator and the freezer are actually being deprived of light as well as warmth. The seeds will get some light whenever the door of the refrigerator or freezer is open, but you should be aware that the second and third pots are not really giving fair results. It is unlikely that the seeds in the freezer will survive the low temperature—once the seeds are defrosted they will probably remain dormant.

Page 27 Wood lice generally prefer a moist, dark environment, such as you would find under a plant pot or a log. You should have found more wood lice in the dark, damp part of the tray.

Page 29 You might not find all the animals that were caught overnight because some might have been eaten by others!

Page 35 You must monitor your ecosystem carefully. If you have too many predators they will soon eat all the other animals. They will then starve to death themselves when they have no more to eat. If there are too few predators the numbers of plant-eating animals will increase.

Page 39 Adding more ladybugs would result in a decrease in the number of aphids. Taking out ladybugs would result in an increase in the number of aphids. Ladybugs are predators and are active insects, often on the move in search of their prey. Aphids are plant eaters. Once they have found a place to feed they don't move around much.

INDEX